Church or Chicken Coop?

Church or Chicken Coop?

A CHOICE FOR AN AARONIC PRIESTHOOD BOY

A Novel Based on Actual Experiences

George D. Durrant

ISBN:978-1-944657-05-5
e. 1

Published by:
Spring Creek Book Company
P.O. Box 1013
Rexburg, ID 83440

www.springcreekbooks.com

Cover design © Spring Creek Book Company

Printed in the United States of America
Printed on acid-free paper

Chapter One

This book is about a young man named George. George is a fun name to say. It sort of starts and ends the same way. I think you'll like George when you get to know him better.

Here is a picture of George and his family. He is identified on the picture by the number 1. Take a good look at him. Nice-looking young fellow, don't you think?

How old do you think George is in this picture?

Before you answer, read what George once said about himself:

- When I became a deacon at age twelve, I was largest deacon in my quorum.
- When I became a teacher at age fourteen, I was the same size as when I was a deacon, and I was the middle size of all the boys in my quorum.
- When I became a priest at age sixteen, I was just slightly bigger than when I was a teacher. At that time, then, I was one of the smallest boys in my quorum.

What do you think? Look at the picture again. Is George twelve years old in this picture—or is he fourteen or sixteen?

The picture was taken so long ago that not even George knows how old he was at the time.

Here are some more questions you can answer by looking at the picture of George and his family.

1. How many brothers did George have?
2. How many sisters?
3. Which one in the picture do you think probably didn't like to go to church? You probably think it's the one who isn't wearing a suit. How did you come up with that answer? Whatever way in which you came up with it, it's the correct answer. He is number 6, and his name is Bill. George's mother wanted all her boys to dress up in suits for this picture, but Bill refused, saying he didn't like wearing a suit.
4. Two other brothers quit attending church during their Aaronic Priesthood days. Which ones do you think they are? One is Kent, number 9; he was an All-Star basketball player. The other brother who stopped going to church is John, number 10. he was a war hero and won the Silver Star metal for bravery.
5. Which one of George's brothers do you think was his bishop when he was a deacon and a teacher? Which

one looks like a bishop to you? That's right: it's Stewart, number 4.

6. There is another brother in the picture named Duane. What number is he? That's right; he's number 5. When George was a deacon, Duane was drafted into the Army. When he got home from the war, he went on a mission to New Zealand.

7. One of George's parents was very religious and never missed church. The other one went to church only when one of the boys was going to go on a mission. Which one of George's parents do you think was the religious one? Here's a hint: she's wearing a necklace George made for her. Why do you think George made such a beautiful necklace for her? That's right. It was because George loved his mother, whose name was Marinda. She and George's two sisters (numbers 7 and 8) "spoiled" George when he was young.

8. Number 3 in the picture is George's father, Bert. Bert said the reason he didn't go to church was because his suit itched. Besides that, he said, "When I came to church my big dog came with me, and the bishop ordered his counselors to take the dog out of the chapel. The dog wasn't barking or nothing like that. So I told the bishop that if the church is too good for my dog, it's too good for me." So he never came back to church.

9. Other than George, then, how many of George's family attended church at the time this picture was taken? Let's count them.

Did number 2 go to church regularly? Yes. That's one *yes*.

Did number 3? No. That's one *no*. Did number 4 go to church regularly? Yes. That's two *yeses*. Did number 5? Yes. That's three *yeses*. Did number 6? No. That's two *nos*. Were George's two sisters, numbers 7 and 8, churchgoers? Yes.

That's five *yeses*. Were the two brothers, numbers 9 and 10, attending church? No and no. That's four *nos*.

Let's see: five of the ten members of George's family did go to church and four did not.

But we didn't count George. I'll tell you this about George: He attended church every Sunday at the time the picture was taken.

But the question is, would he keep doing so?

We'll find out as we read this book.

Now you know quite a bit about George and his family. You know that he was the youngest of the eight children. You know was that his oldest brother, Stewart, was his bishop during his junior high/Aaronic Priesthood years. You know that two of his brothers were very religious and three were not. You know his mother was very religious and his father was not.

Now, considering you don't know about George, do you think he will keep going to church as he goes through junior and senior high school? Or do you think he won't?

If you think George will continue faithful as a deacon, teacher, and priest, do you also think he will someday become an elder, go on a mission, get married in the temple, and continue faithful in the Church as an adult? Or do you think he won't?

So, what do you think so far? Will George be faithful like two of his brothers, or will he fall away from the Church like his other two brothers? That's a hard question to answer, isn't it? You'll need more information before you decide. You'll need to know the thoughts of George's mind and the feelings of his heart. You'll also need to know how he behaved from age twelve to age sixteen and into his adult years.

You'll need to know George's story.

Chapter Two

Let's look at part of George's story.

When George was a young boy, Primary was held on Tuesday afternoon right after elementary school. At that time George assumed school wasn't an option. He assumed he had no choice about whether to go to school. He felt the same way about Primary.

Because of that, George seldom ever missed Primary. He walked with some of his friends the quarter of a mile from the elementary school to the Fourth Ward meetinghouse. George didn't mind going to Primary, because when he got there he and his friends played "Pomp Pomp Pull-Away" or "Red Rover, Red Rover, Send George Right Over." They played on the front lawn until the teachers called George and the others into the building for religious instruction.

Looking back on the whole thing, which happened many years ago, George cannot recall the lessons he learned in those Primary classes.

However, when George got older, there were some things he knew about Jesus, Heavenly Father, prayer, and how to be a good boy. He couldn't remember when he learned them, but he knew he probably learned about those things in Primary, in Sunday school, and from his mother.

During the last two years of George's time in Primary, he had perfect attendance. As a reward, he was honored during sacrament meeting, where he was presented a Book of

Mormon. George's mother was deeply proud of that accomplishment.

George remembers how sad he was when his meetinghouse burned to the ground during his next-to-last year of Primary. For the next three years, his ward had to hold all their meetings in the basement of the big American Fork Tabernacle. Sadly, there was no place on the Tabernacle grounds to play "Pomp Pomp Pull-Away" or "Red Rover, Red Rover, Send George Right Over."

During George's last year of Primary in a classroom in the basement of that Tabernacle, George had an experience he will never forget. His teacher, Laura Timpson, taught a most interesting lesson. Here's what George remembers about that lesson:

> I can remember as plain as if it were yesterday every word that this beloved teacher taught that day. She told the story of a young man named Joseph Smith.
>
> Using all my memory power, I can truly say that up until that time, I had never heard of Joseph Smith.
>
> That day, I remember Sister Timpson telling us about Joseph Smith walking to a grove of trees near his home. There, in the trees, he knelt and prayed. In that prayer, he asked God which church was true.
>
> As I listened, my teacher continued the story by saying, "When Joseph prayed, he saw a light coming down through the trees. Then he saw Heavenly Father and Jesus standing in the light."
>
> Sister Timpson kept going. "Joseph asked Heavenly Father and Jesus which church was true. Jesus told him none of the churches were true, but

that He would reveal the true church to Joseph Smith."

I wondered what other churches there were. I had heard of Protestants and Catholics, but I didn't know exactly what those words meant. Then, for the first time, I wondered, "Is the church I go to the one that came from Joseph Smith, and is it the true church?"

My teacher continued, "Three years later an angel appeared to Joseph Smith in his bedroom. This angel was named Moroni."

She said, "The angel Moroni told Joseph that in a hill nearby Joseph's home, there were some golden plates that were buried in the ground. The angel told Joseph that someday he was going to get those golden plates and translate them from a strange language into English. And what he would translate would become The Book of Mormon."

So that was the first time George had ever heard of Joseph Smith. It was also the first time he knew the origin of the Book of Mormon.

George continued his story:

I thought about those things as I walked home from Primary that day. But the next day I did not think much about what the teacher had said. As an eleven-year-old boy, I had other things to think about, and I never really thought much about "true churches" or things like that.

George didn't personally know anyone in town who was not a member of the same church as he was. Because of that, he never had to explain his point of view. Besides, as far as

George could remember at that stage of his life, he really didn't have a point of view about religious stuff.

So, dear reader, considering what you just read, do you think George had a strong enough testimony to be worthy to become a deacon when he turned twelve years old?

Chapter Three

Not only did George not have a testimony of the restoration of the gospel, but he also didn't pay tithing. Here's what George had to say about that:

> At age eleven, I didn't know anything about tithing. I don't even know if my mom and dad paid tithing. I don't think my dad paid tithing. I'm sure my mom would've paid it if she could've figured out what 10 percent of nothing was. Because she never did earn any money. I'm sure my brother Stewart, who was the bishop, paid tithing, because he had to ask every adult in his ward if they did.
>
> But he never asked me if I paid tithing, even though I worked in the summer thinning beats and weeding onions for Draper Giles. I earned twenty-five cents an hour, but I never did pay tithing on those earnings. I probably would've if someone had told me to, but neither my mother nor my bishop brother asked me to.

What do you think? Should George have become a deacon if he didn't pay tithing?

But while we're judging George's worthiness to become a deacon, we should know one thing he did that was right.

He lived the Word of Wisdom when he was eleven years old. Somehow, he did know that members of The Church of Jesus Christ of Latter-day Saints didn't smoke tobacco or drink alcohol or coffee.

His mother often told him never to do those things, and his Primary teachers taught him those same things.

But there was one exception to his obedience to the Word of Wisdom. George had this to say about that:

> I could tell my mom didn't want my dad to smoke or to drink the wine he made from his grapes. He kept the wine down in the cellar. When my Uncle Walt came to visit, they always went down the stairs to the cellar. I could always see that when they came up the stairs from the cellar, they were happier than when they went down.

So George's father was not a good example to him when it came to living The Word of Wisdom.

George remembers that there was only one time when he was eleven years old that he disobeyed the Word of Wisdom:

> When I was eleven my father took me with him up American Fork Canyon to hunt deer. I was excited to be included with my father and his brothers at the deer hunt campgrounds.
>
> We all slept in tents. In the morning we got up before daybreak. It was very cold. We made a bonfire, and my dad made a big pot of coffee. Everybody got a tin cup and filled it with coffee. I thought the coffee sure did smell good. My dad looked at me and told me to get a cup. I got it, and he poured my cup half full. He told me to put a lot of cream and sugar in it.

I wasn't sure I should be drinking coffee. But my mother wasn't there, so it didn't seem to be all that wrong. It sure did taste good, and it made me feel warm all over.

So that was the only time George broke the Word of Wisdom. But he did break it.

His brother, the bishop, wasn't there on that deer hunt, so he didn't know George had sipped on a cup of coffee. And George never did tell his mother that he had done that. So not telling her that he had done that was kind of a lie. At least he didn't tell his mother or anyone else the truth.

What do you think? Should George, who broke the Word of Wisdom, have been ordained a deacon later that month?

On the other hand, George did attend church every week with his mother when he was eleven years old. She had to walk to church alone, so George always walked with her. George loved his mother and was always nice and kind to her.

So That's pretty good, don't you think?

Maybe he should be a deacon.

Having read this book so far, you know quite a bit about George. You also know that deacons are pretty good young men. To do the sacred things they do, such as passing the sacrament, they have to be worthy.

What do you think? Should George become a deacon? If he becomes a deacon, do you think he will keep coming to church and became a teacher and a priest like two of his brothers did? Or will he lose interest and drop out like his other two brothers did?

Chapter Four

Knowing all that you now know about George, could you sustain him to become a deacon?

Well, on October 24,1943, George Donald Durrant became a deacon in The Church of Jesus Christ of Latter-day Saints.

This is how that all happened as George remembers it:

It was a cold October day as I walked up the Old Mill Lane coming from school. When I was just two blocks from home I got quite excited because I liked home a lot better than I liked school. I also thought that maybe mother would give me a present for my birthday.

I walked so fast during the last block that I was almost running when I reached the front gate. I hurried onto the porch and opened the front door. I looked across the room where my mother stood stirring some soup on the old coal stove. She turned her head toward me and announced, "Happy twelfth birthday!"

She put the spoon down and hurried across the room to me. She put her hands on my shoulders, looked into my eyes, and said, "I have got a birthday present for you, George."

I smiled broadly with excitement as she led me by the arm to our big round kitchen table. I saw a box wrapped in brown paper. I wondered what it was.

She handed me a pair of scissors, and I cut the strings that bound the paper together. I quickly unwrapped the paper and saw a cardboard box. I threw the top of the box over my shoulder and was greatly disappointed when I saw that she had bought me some kind of navy-blue coat.

I had hoped for an erector set or a magic set or some other kind of toy. But it was clothes. And I wasn't too interested in getting new clothes.

Sensing my disappointment, my mother took the coat out of the package and held it up for me to see as she said, "I've bought you a new suit because this Sunday morning you will become a deacon in The Church of Jesus Christ of Latter-day Saints, and you will get to pass the sacrament. When you do, you'll be able to wear this new suit. Won't that be exciting?"

I wasn't too enthusiastic about the whole thing. She said, "Here are the trousers. And I also bought you a new white shirt and a tie. Just think how handsome you will look when you pass the sacrament in a navy-blue suit."

She then excitedly told me to go to my bedroom and put on the trousers and the white shirt. She said, "I'll keep the coat here. I think I know how to tie a tie, so I'll help you tie your tie when you get back."

I went to the bedroom, put on the trousers and the shirt, and went back to my mother. She taught me how to tie the tie. Then she held the suit coat so I could put one arm in and then the other.

Everything seemed to fit pretty well.

I wanted to look in a mirror to see how I looked, but we had no mirror big enough for that. My mother stood back a few feet and looked at me with tears of joy in her eyes. I could tell by her expression that I looked really good in my new navy-blue suit.

She said, "Oh, George you look so handsome. You look like a young priesthood boy."

While I was still dressed in my new suit, my brother Kent came home from high school and saw me in all his splendor. He said, "You look pretty good in that. Did Mom get that for you because you're going to be a deacon?" Without waiting for an answer, he continued, "She got me one like that when I was going to be a deacon. I grew so fast that it only fit me for a year. After that I never did get another suit."

Then Kent said, "I didn't like wearing those kinds of clothes. That's one of the reasons I quit going to church. Mom told me she'd get me another one, but I knew those things cost a lot of money. I told her she didn't need to get me a new one because I'd never wear it if she did. I just didn't like church the way she did. None of my friends went, so I quit going."

Then Kent kind of sobered as he said, "I'm glad you go. Mom needs somebody to go there with her."

George had wondered why Kent had quit going to church. He knew their mom tried getting him to go each week, but he was very stubborn. He always refused, saying he was too tired and that he would try to go next week and things like that.

George had never considered not going to church. However, because he tried to do everything just like Kent did, he wondered how it would be to just sleep in and then get up and spend the morning reading the Sunday newspaper sports page and comics section. He thought, *That would kinda be nice, but it sure would make my mother sad.*

Besides that, George thought, *if I don't go to church, I won't get to see my friend Herbie Pawlowski who is always there.*

After Kent went out to milk the family cow, George went to his bedroom, took off his new Sunday clothes, and put on his corduroy trousers and his polo T-shirt. These clothes were a lot more comfortable than the suit and tie.

He then went out to the chicken coops to gather the eggs that had been laid that day. He had done this chore every day for as long as he could remember.

After taking the two wire baskets filled with eggs down into the cellar, he walked out to the barn where Kent had finished milking and was playing basketball with his friends.

George hoped that one of the friends would not show up so there would be a chance for him to be on one of the teams. George liked basketball more than anything in the whole world. His greatest dream was that someday he would grow tall like Kent and be a star like Kent was becoming.

That night at supper George was pleased to see a birthday cake with twelve candles on it. When Kent came to the table and saw the cake, he said, "Oh, no. I forgot it was George's birthday. If I had remembered, I would've bought him a new bicycle."

The next night, which was a Saturday, George's mother insisted that he take his weekly bath. As he stepped into the warm water, his mother shouted, "Scrub yourself well, George. Deacons need to be real clean."

The next morning, George's mother helped him put on his new clothes. She even helped him comb his hair, which he seldom did. She made a "part" in it and combed it in two different directions as she said, "Deacons always comb their hair real nice and look their very best."

George looked in the mirror and kinda liked the way his hair looked. When he came into the kitchen where his dad, Bert, was seated in the corner of the room in his rocking chair. His dad looked up from the newspaper, smiled, and nodded his head in approval. Bert never did say much to George, so it was a real treat for the young boy to win his father's acclaim.

His mother remarked, "I cooked you two eggs instead of one. A priesthood man needs to have a good breakfast on Sunday."

After breakfast, Bert opened the door to Kent's bedroom and shouted, "Come on. Get up. If you're not going to go to church, you can help me clean out chicken coops,"

George was happy he was going to church and wouldn't have to shovel chicken manure.

A few minutes later, George, kinda feeling good in his Sunday attire, left the house holding his mother's hand to walk the half mile to the Old Fourth Ward meetinghouse.

Herbie was waiting at the door of the church to greet George. George sat next to his mother. and Herbie took the next seat over.

Bishop Durrant, George's older brother, stood at the pulpit and said, "Today is Herbie Pawlowski's birthday. He turns twelve today. And my brother George turned twelve on Friday. So they're both old enough to be deacons. Would you two boys please stand up?"

He then said, "These two fine young men are old enough to be deacons. I know they're both good fellows who don't swear or smoke tobacco or drink alcohol. So I propose that they be ordained deacons. All those who can sustain George and Herbie to become deacons, please raise your right hand."

George felt good at his name being called out like that and everybody voting for him. He knew that if he ran for any kind of office over at school, nobody would vote for him. But here in the church they all did.

After that meeting, everyone went to their Sunday school class. George and Herbie didn't go, though, because the bishop invited them to come to his office to be ordained deacons. Both of Herbie's parents were there. And George's mother was there too. But George's father was not there.

The bishop spoke to the little group about how important it was for a boy to become a deacon. When he was finished, he said, "George, take this seat here, and I will lay my hands upon your head, and by the authority of the priesthood and in the name of Jesus Christ I will ordain you a deacon."

George humbly walked to the chair and sat down. He felt the bishop's hands on his head. As the bishop said the words that conferred upon him the Aaronic Priesthood and ordained him to be a deacon, George felt he was sort of floating. He didn't know what the feelings he felt were, but he knew it was something different than he had ever felt before. It was like his head was being pushed down but his shoulders were rising.

After the bishop said "Amen," he shook George's hand and said, "Go give your mother a big hug. She's proud of you." As George moved toward his mother, he could see tears falling down her cheeks. George could also feel that his own eyes were a little wet. It wasn't because he was sad. It was because he felt so happy that his heart pushed the tears into his eyes.

A few minutes later, Herbie had also received the great honor of becoming a deacon.

Chapter Five

After Sunday school was over, everyone started coming back into the chapel for sacrament meeting. The bishop approached George and Herbie and said, "The deacons who were supposed to pass the sacrament snuck out of church early. I would like you two to take their places."

Herbie smiled broadly in agreement because he didn't mind making mistakes in front of other people. But George, who couldn't bear to have people see him looking dumb, remembers having different feelings:

When the bishop told us what he wanted us to do, I was scared. I didn't know how to pass the sacrament. I'd seen the other deacons do it. But they knew how, and I didn't. In a panic, I told my brother, "I can't do that."

He replied, "George, you are a deacon now. When Heavenly Father wants you to do something, you can do it. So go up there and sit there in front of the sacrament table. You'll be able to do it. Don't worry; the Lord will tell you how"

I wanted to leave church early like the other deacons had, but my mother was watching me, and I couldn't scoot out the door. I sat with Herbie. My hands were trembling. My tie felt like it was choking me. Suddenly I knew why Kent didn't want to wear a suit and a tie and do hard stuff like this. In a frenzy I wondered, *When do we stand up, and where do we go when we get the trays?*

Everybody sang the sacrament song. I didn't sing. I was too nervous to sing or do anything else. Finally, one of the priests knelt and said the prayer on the sacrament bread. Herbie and I still just sat there. The other priest beckoned us to come forward. We stood and we walked two steps toward the table.

One of the priests handed Herbie a bread tray. The other priest handed me one too.

For some reason, once the tray was in my hand, I suddenly felt calm inside. I said to myself, *I can do this.* My hand gripped the sacrament tray more firmly than I had when I first held it. I straightened my shoulders and lifted my chin and stood up a bit straighter. I knew everybody in the room was looking at me, but for some reason that didn't scare me like it usually did.

I looked over at my mother, who was looking at me. I had never seen her glow so much as she did then. I turned and looked at the first row and decided I'd start there. I gripped the tray tighter and walked across to the end of the front row.

Herbie, who had first gone up to the rostrum, placed the tray in front of the bishop so that he could be the first to partake.

From there, I could see out of the corner of my eye that Herbie was now headed over to the side rows of seats. He was smiling. Seeing him doing that made me smile. I didn't know if deacons were supposed to smile when they were passing the sacrament. But I was feeling good and couldn't help it.

I put the tray in front a nice lady and she had the honor of being the first person to whom I had ever passed the sacrament. She took a piece of bread and looked up at me and smiled. Then I handed her the tray, and she passed it to the person sitting next to her. I circled around and went to the other side, where I waited for the tray. I received it and sent it back the other way. Then I went to the opposite side to receive the tray there.

Somehow, I just knew where to go next. I could see that Herbie was doing an equally magnificent job.

Finally, Herbie and I both knew simultaneously that everyone in the congregation had partaken of the sacrament.

I nodded to Herbie. The two of us strode side by side back to the sacrament table. I had never loved Herbie as much as I did at that moment. I said to myself, *I think I am the best Deacon in the church, and I think Herbie is second.*

Back at the sacrament table, one of the priests took my tray and held it up for me to take one of the remaining pieces of bread. It tasted really good.

I glanced over and saw my mother, and she nodded at me.

Herbie and I sat down, and the other priest said the prayer on the water. We did exactly the same thing we had done in passing the bread. Everyone in the room had the privilege of taking the sacrament because of Herbie and me.

After sacrament meeting was over, I met my mother at the door. I held her hand as we walked down the stairs to the sidewalk. As we begin the journey home, she held my hand tightly and exclaimed, "George I was so proud of you. I was fearful you might not know where to go. Did the bishop explain to you where you should go and what you should do?"

I replied, "The bishop didn't tell us anything. I just had these feelings about what I was supposed to do and where I was supposed to go, and I did it."

My mother squeezed my hand as she said, "You look so handsome doing your priesthood duty. The new suit fit you so perfectly. Your tie was tied just right. Your hair was so well groomed. When I looked at you, the Lord put a feeling into my heart that told me, 'Your son it is a priesthood man.'"

As we continued to walk and talk, my mother asked me if I knew the reason why we partake of the sacrament. I told her I did not. She tried to explain it to me. But I still didn't understand. All I knew was that I sure did feel happy when I was going from person to person passing the sacrament.

So that is the story of the first time George passed the sacrament. He did all that while his brother Kent was home cleaning out a chicken coop. Do you think George will keep going to church or will he drop out like Kent did?

If he keeps having those good feelings he had when he was passing the sacrament, I think he will stick with it. Don't you think?

Chapter Six

For the next two years, George never missed going to sacrament meeting with his mother. He was glad that he could make her happy by being her "church-going friend."

Meanwhile, during the same two years, George was struggling over at junior high school. You see, George was not the smartest boy in the seventh and eighth grade. He was smart enough, but his mind often wandered, and sometimes he talked to his friends when he should've been listening to the teacher.

His favorite class was physical education. He and his friends called it *gym*.

George liked that class because playing sports was his favorite thing. He wanted to be like his brother Kent, who was now on the varsity basketball team even though he was only in the tenth grade.

George had hoped he would be the best athlete in seventh grade, but he found out in gym class that there were other boys who were now bigger than him, stronger than him, faster than him, and more skilled than him. And even the average kids at school were as good as him at sports.

When he realized that, George began to feel inferior to the other boys. After all, he was Kent Durrant's brother, and he was supposed to be a good athlete. And he wasn't. These realizations caused George to feel inferior. He lost his confidence, and he became timid. No other successes could compensate for the fact that he was not the star of his gym class.

Besides that, in his mind he didn't have any other successes except in his mother's eyes. Maybe he had some successes over at church while passing the sacrament and doing stuff like that. But that was not as important to him as being successful over at school.

However, during those years, he sometimes felt that passing the sacrament was the most important thing in the world.

George's social life centered on his friendship with other boys who wanted to be and were good athletes. Some of these boys swore and used other bad words so they could look tough. George had also heard Kent use some of those words.

George thought he might be a better athlete if he used those words. But he knew it was wrong to talk that way when his brother was the bishop, and he knew his mother would be disappointed and sad if she found out he said those things. So he didn't. But he often wondered if he should.

George seldom saw Herbie at school. That's because even though he and Herbie were the same age, Herbie was in a grade behind George in school.

Herbie did not want to be an athlete and didn't even like to talk about sports. He was not popular. He often sat alone in the lunchroom eating sandwiches that he brought from home. George and his friends always bought the school lunch and sat together and talked and laughed.

Sometimes George said hello to Herbie as he passed by him. Other times he just looked the other way like he didn't even see Herbie. George hoped that Herbie didn't feel bad being ignored. He wanted to be friendly to Herbie, but even more, he wanted to be with the athletic and popular kids.

George's mother didn't know that George ignored Herbie at school. He never told her. George was sort of in between what he wanted to be and who he really was.

However, each Sunday at church Herbie was once again George's very best friend. Herbie was very respectful of all the teachers at church. George sometimes liked to goof off during Sunday school classes, but Herbie was not good at goofing off. George tried to be as respectful as Herbie.

At school, some of George's friends tried to be funny by talking about girls and talking to girls. During those times, George always kept silent. He wanted to say something, but he was too shy.

However, there was one girl George really liked. Her name was Louise. He had liked her all through elementary school. She was always kind and said hello to him. It was hard for George to say hello back. He'd just duck his head and almost whisper, "Hello." He felt he was not important enough to say anymore to such an important girl.

George thought she was the prettiest girl in the world. But he never talked to anyone other than himself about her. He never mentioned her to a friend or to his mother. His feelings about her were his big secret. It made him happy to think about her and to remember that she said hello to him every day.

George told the following story about his shyness:

One day I was helping Kent and some of his friends paint our family's house.

These older guys often made fun of me. I guess I had big ears, and they—not Kent, but the others—called me "Ears." This taunting hurt me deep inside, but I never said anything back to them.

When we were painting the house, a girl from my school class named Eva June rode her bike up the Alpine Road. She turned at Seventh North, passed the mailboxes, and came right up to our front gate. I recognized her and wondered why she had stopped at our house.

Kent and his friends watched her approach and wondered what was going on. As soon as I recognized who she was, I didn't look at her anymore. I hoped she would get on her bike and ride away.

I nearly died of a heart attack when she called out, "I came to talk to you, George."

Kent's friends started shouting, "Hey, Ears, go talk to her. She's your girlfriend." Having them call me "Ears" and having that girl waiting for me to come out to her were two hard blows all at the same time. I just wished the earth would open up and swallow me.

The guys started shouting, "Get out there, Ears. Your girlfriend's waiting for you." They were all laughing and stuff like that.

I could not bear it and immediately went in the house. I left Eva June leaning against her bicycle at the front gate. I watched out the window. After a few minutes, she climbed on her bike and went on her way.

Inside the house, I felt so bad. I laid on my bed looking up at the ceiling, trying not to cry. Because eighth-graders don't cry,

George felt worse than he had ever felt before. He felt sorry for Eva June, because he knew how bad she felt.

After telling this story, he added, "I wanted to be different than how I was in that story, but I didn't have the courage to do so. I knew deacons weren't supposed to smoke or drink or say bad words. But I knew there was something worse than those things, and that was the way I treated Eva June."

Chapter Seven

There was another girl named Lela May, and most of the kids in junior high thought that Lela May was the prettiest girl in the school. Even Kent and his friends who were in high school liked the looks of Lela May.

George never talked about who was pretty and who wasn't. But he knew Lela May was pretty, all right. But to him the prettiest girl in the junior high—in fact, in the whole town and in the whole world—was Louise.

But Louise was not in George's ward, and Lela May was. So each week at church George not only saw Herbie, but he also saw Lela May.

At school she was always surrounded by boys. When George walked by, she hardly noticed him.

But at church she was very friendly to him, and he could tell she liked him better than she liked Herbie. That was the first time George ever felt that any girl liked him better than she liked someone else. He was too shy to say a whole lot to Lela May, but he could say more to her than he could ever say to Louise.

One day she even walked up to where George was sitting waiting for Sunday school to begin, and she sat by him. The congregation started singing the opening song. Lela May opened the songbook to the right number and held it up so George could see it, but he did not sing.

When Lela May saw that George was not singing, she commanded him, "Sing."

George replied, "I can't tell what words they are singing. I sing the first line and start to sing the second line, but everyone else is singing something else."

Lela may could tell what he was doing. She told him, as she pointed to the page, "You sing this first line. Then you go down and sing the first line down here and keep doing that to the end of the song. Then you come back and sing the second line and go down from there."

When she saw that George seemed to understand, she said, "We are right here on this word. So sing."

For the first time, George sang all the verses. When the song was over, Lela May looked at him and smiled. She was the first girl who had ever paid enough attention to him to talk to him about how to do something.

George liked her. But the girl he liked best of all was still Louise. From then on, George went to church because his mother wanted him to and because he got to see Herbie there. But when he got to church, the thing he liked best was that Lela May was there.

When George passed the sacrament, he always tried to pass it to the row of people where Lela May was sitting with her mother. That is why when he went to church he made sure his hair was combed and his tie was tied just right.

George was discovering that church was more than he had supposed.

He looked at his brother, the bishop, and knew the church was a place of respect.

He looked at his mother and knew the church was a place of love.

He looked at Herbie and knew the church was a place of friendship.

He looked at Lela May and knew the church was a place to be nice like he was to Herbie, and like Lela May was to him.

He thought of Louise and wished she could be there to see him in a suit and tie, standing tall and straight and passing the sacrament—a priesthood man. *Surely then*, he thought, *she would think of me as I think of her.*

So now you know a lot more about George. Do you think he'll keep coming to church and become a teacher and a priest? Or do you think will he lose interest and follow Kent and some of the other boys at school and dean out chicken coups and do other fun things on Sunday?

Before you answer, you have to realize that Lela May was really pretty, and George knew it.

So, what do you think? Will George keep hanging in there by being a faithful churchgoer?

Chapter Eight

The summer before George turned fourteen years old, old enough to become a teacher in the Aaronic Priesthood, he came to an unexpected crossroads in his life. Here's how George remembers that critical experience:

> My father never took me to church, but I can't complain, because he often took me fishing. I hate to admit it, but at that time I liked going fishing better than I liked attending church.
>
> On the Fourth of July, my father—I called him *Dad*—said to my older brother Kent and me, "You boys dig some worms." That was his way of telling us we were going fishing.
>
> We knew right where there some nice juicy worms. Within fifteen minutes we had a tin can nearly full.
>
> My older brother Stewart (my bishop) had been in on the earlier planning of the fishing trip with my dad, so he drove up to our place at about three that afternoon. When Kent and I spotted him coming, we ran out to the car with our fishing gear and piled into the backseat with our fishing poles sticking out of the open window. Dad soon joined us, and we were off on our journey to the South Fork of the Provo River.

After an hour's drive, we rented a little cabin under the pine trees, close to the river's rushing water. Half an hour later we were at the stream's edge, hoping there were some trout waiting to eat a tasty worm.

An hour later, neither of us had even had a nibble on our line, and our patience was wearing thin. We started losing interest in fishing and decided to go on a walk across a large field of newly mown hay.

I didn't mind that we hadn't caught any fish, because fishing wasn't my favorite thing. My favorite thing was being with my brother.

The winding river made a big U-turn, so we were soon on the banks of the same river, just a little farther up the stream.

Without even talking about it, each one of us simultaneously picked up one of the flattest of the two million rocks that lined the river's edge and threw it so it would skip one or two or maybe even three times along the top of the water.

Soon tiring of that, we found some empty beer bottles that had been left there earlier by some really happy fishermen. We took turns throwing them upstream; as they came bobbing along the waves, we bombarded them like they were enemy ships, shattering them into thousands of pieces. Our shouting at each successful strike and laughing in between made everyone along the river wonder what was causing the excitement.

Little did they know that the discarded beer bottles had brought happiness to two separate groups—the beer drinkers and the beer bottle busters.

Pretty soon the beer bottles were all gone, and our arms were tired from throwing things. We made our way back to a large log and sat there side by side. We just sat there silently watching the dark-then-white, swirling, deep water pass us by.

Kent broke the silence by saying, "I'm pretty nervous about the basketball season coming up in a few months. The folks of American Fork think that I'm going to lead the team to the first state championship American Fork has ever won. I sure hope I can do that, but there are a lot of good teams in the state."

I said, "There's no way anybody could beat our team with you playing. You're six-foot-seven and you are the best darn player this state has ever had."

Looking out at the river, Kent nodded his head as if to agree without bragging. Then he turned his head, looked at me, and asked, "Do you want to play basketball?"

"Yeah, I want to be half as good as you are, which would make me the second-best player in school history—next to you, of course."

Sensing my desires and wondering if it could ever happen, Kent asked, "You're in the eighth grade now, aren't you? How tall are you now?"

I shyly replied with a surge of guilt, "I'm just five-foot-seven."

"Man!" Kent replied. Then he asked, "When are you going to grow?" Without waiting for me to answer, he continued, "When I was your age, I was six-foot-five."

Neither of us said anything for a few minutes. Feeling bad, as I always did when I thought about not being able to grow, I picked up a big rock, held it over my head, walked over to the river, threw it into the water with both hands, registering my inward pain and bitterness over not being able to grow.

I explained to Kent something I had never said to anybody else: "I don't even like to shower at school at the end of gym class because a lot of the guys my age are turning into men, and I'm still a little boy. That makes me embarrassed. It makes me sadder than anything else in my life."

Kent didn't seem to feel sorry for me as he said, "Yeah, I sure was glad I developed into a man when I was in the seventh grade. But don't worry about it. Someday you'll probably grow. I'll bet you'll become at least six feet tall."

Almost before the last word was out of his mouth, I replied, "I don't want to just be six feet tall. I want to be six-foot-seven like you. I want to be like you in every way."

Kent seemed a little bit surprised by my outburst and replied, "I appreciate that, George. But there are other things besides sports. You'll be a better man than me."

Because I admired him so much I was hurt by his words. I almost shouted, "Nobody will ever be a better man than Kent Durrant."

"You're already a better man than me, George. You're a religious guy. You like going to church. Me, I don't like doing that. I don't see any sense in wasting my time over there when I'd sooner be somewhere else. When I don't go to Sunday school and that, dad makes me clean out the chicken coop. But I'd sooner do that than go to church and listen to boring talks and boring lessons. I'm just not interested in that kind of stuff. I don't want to pass the sacrament and stuff like that." Then he looked at me and asked, "Do you like doing that kind of stuff?"

Before I even thought of an answer, I felt a little ashamed, and replied, "I kinda like doing that, but I've been thinking maybe I could at least miss church some of the time. Then I could help you clean out the chicken coop."

Kent stared at me until I had to look back. Then he said, "Don't talk like that. If you didn't go to church, it would break Mom's heart. I know it makes her cry when I tell her I don't want to go to church. But I can't live my life just to please her. She likes going to church and she thinks I should too, but I don't."

I felt all confused and didn't know what to say. So I just sat there looking at the river and thinking.

Kent then said, "Some of my friends have quit going to church too. The only ones who go the church are those who seem like 'mama's boys'— kind of sissies, not the tough guys."

When I didn't answer him right off, Kent suggested, "You don't have to follow their example. And you don't have to follow mine. You just have to decide for yourself. Is it really worth going to church or not?"

With that he stood up and announced, "It's getting a little bit dark. We'd better head back to our cabin."

I was glad to go back, because whenever I was alone in the dark, I was scared. But when I was with Kent, nothing scared me, because I reckoned he could fight off a mountain lion or a monster or a maniac or anything else.

That night as I lay in my bed, I could hear the stream running by. The soothing sound of the stream running by in the mountains usually made me fall asleep before I even knew it. But that night I had a hard time going to sleep. I wondered what I would decide when I decided for myself whether or not to be a religious guy.

As George lay there unable to sleep, his mind jumped from one thought to another.

He remembered that during junior high he still didn't have what his mother referred to as a "testimony." He went to church, but he didn't go because of any burning desire in his heart. He went because it was the thing to do. It was like going to school or something like that.

On the other hand, he thought, he really did like passing the sacrament with Herbie at his side. And sometimes he liked the talks a little bit, and the lessons were kinda interesting at times.

He smiled up at the ceiling of the canvas tent where they slept outside the cabin. He knew there was something above the top of the tent and even higher than the mountains. A surge of joy caused him to almost shudder as he somehow knew that he would soon be a teacher in the Aaronic Priesthood.

As a teacher in the Aaronic Priesthood, George knew that he and Herbie would have the duty of preparing the bread and water for the sacrament. If he and Herbie didn't do it, George wondered, who would? He even considered that the people who went to church might not have the sacrament if he and Herbie didn't show up.

Maybe, George said to himself, *maybe someday I'll drop out of the church. But not now. Not now.*

Finally, George drifted off to sleep.

Chapter Nine

A few months later, George and Herbie were ordained teachers in the Aaronic Priesthood on the same day.

George recalled:

> Herbie and I had new duties now. We had to get to church early and prepare the sacrament trays with bread and water.
>
> In those days the sacrament trays seemed to be made of real metal and shined like silver. And the cups were not made of cardboard or plastic; they were made of real thin glass. They were the teeniest glasses ever made, and they sparkled like diamonds.
>
> The sacrament trays were round, and the cups were lined up in rings like the circles in a target.
>
> To put the water in the cups, we filled a pitcher with cold water. Then we had a little contraption made of metal and shaped like a hand with four little fingers. We poured water in the "palm" part of that thing and then tilted it so the water would flow down into four miniature glasses. Then we moved it and did the same thing until all the anxious little receptacles were filled with water.
>
> Herbie and I loved doing that. We felt like we shouldn't get a single drop of water on any of those

shining trays. If we did, we took a piece of cloth and quickly wiped up our spill.

After church, the ladies in the ward took the little glass glasses and the silver trays home and sparkled them all up again for the next week.

George also had the duty of bringing bread each week for the sacrament. His mother baked bread, so the family never had to buy bread at the store. Each Sunday she sliced off two big pieces of bread, wrapped them in waxed paper, and handed them to George as he went out the door to church. George thought the people who partook of the sacrament thought that bread tasted better than any bread they had ever tasted. He knew that when he and Herbie got their piece, he wished all bread tasted that good.

George remembered more about preparing the sacrament:

Putting the water in the little glasses and the unbroken bread on the trays to be broken by the priests made me feel like I was doing something really important. It made me happy. I can't explain why, because I didn't know then how sacred the sacrament was.

Sometimes we were still working on our sacrament duties when people came into the chapel. Sometimes I could see Lela May sitting there looking up at me and Herbie. I mean, she looked at me a lot more than she looked at Herbie. It made me happy to have her admiring me like that.

My only regret was that I wished it was Louise instead of Lela May. But I liked Lela May a little bit too. Just not as much as I liked Louise. But I never did tell anybody—not even Herbie or my mom or anybody else—that I kinda liked girls a little bit.

Our ward was real small, so there weren't very many Aaronic Priesthood boys. We had some others that were deacons and teachers, but they didn't come to church, at least not regularly. Because of that, Herbie and I still got to pass the sacrament, even after we were teachers. My blue suit still fit me. So I still looked pretty sharp walking around with the sacrament trays, standing up straight, taking the trays to people so that they could partake of the little pieces of bread and little cups of water that Herbie and I had prepared.

I wondered why Kent didn't like doing stuff like that. I supposed that was because everybody is kinda different in what they like and don't like.

Well, what do you think? George is feeling pretty good about the church. Do you agree that he'll probably stick with it, at least for a while?

Chapter Ten

George continued telling his story:

I kept going to church when I was in the ninth grade. I think I decided for myself to do that. But I did see that my mother gave me a lot bigger piece of pie at Sunday dinner because I had just gotten home from church.

But that wasn't the only reason I liked going to church. It was just one of the reasons. There were other reasons; I liked to see Herbie and Lela May. I also liked to make my mother happy. And I wanted to make sure everybody could partake of the sacrament.

And then there was just something inside that I really can't explain. But whatever it was, it made me want to go to church.

Then George remembered a time during this period when a real crisis came into his spiritual life. Here's how he described that situation:

As I said, I was raised on a chicken farm. My job was to gather the eggs two times a day. My father couldn't afford to pay me on a regular basis. Instead he just gave me money when I absolutely needed it. I hated asking him for money, because he was kind of ornery when he had to dig deep into his overalls pocket to find his little black purse. Once he had snapped it open, he carefully and grudgingly counted out the few nickels, dimes, and quarters necessary to meet my request.

As I gathered the eggs one afternoon, I saw two brown hens that had somehow immigrated into our all-white chicken flock. About that same time, I reached in to one of the nests and pulled out six white eggs and one brown one.

That sparked an idea in my mind. What if my father would allow me to keep every brown egg I gathered? I got to thinking that if I could acquire ten more brown hens to live with my father's white hens, they would lay at least six eggs each day. That meant they would lay three dozen eggs each week.

I calculated that I could sell each dozen for twenty-five cents. That meant I would profit by about seventy-five cents each week. With that kind of money, I would not have to ask my father ever again to dig money out of his purse for me.

That night as my father sat reading the daily newspaper, I timidly approached him with my proposition. I asked him if I could get some more brown chickens and let them run loose with his chickens, and then I could have the money for the brown eggs so that he would no longer have to listen to my nickel-and-dime requests.

I was shocked when he replied, "If that's what you want."

Seeming to like the idea of my not constantly asking him for money, he added, "You can go over to Arnold Conder's farm and ask him to sell you a dozen brown eggs that have been fertilized by one of his roosters. When you get the eggs, you can put them under one of the white hens that sits in the nest all day wishing she could be a mother."

He continued, "In twenty-eight days you should have a dozen little chicks. When the little ones grow up, we will eat the roosters and you can keep the hens. We'll keep doing that until you have at least twelve brown laying hens."

In less than a year I was the proud owner of twelve of the prettiest brown hens you've ever seen. I loved gathering the eggs, hoping that in each nest I would find a nice brown egg.

I sold the eggs to all my neighbors for twenty-five cents a dozen. I was now profiting to the tune of seventy-five cents each week.

I tell you of this financial venture because of something that happened to me because of my newly acquired wealth. Way back then, we went to Sunday school in the morning. And then we went back in the early evening to sacrament meeting.

One Sunday afternoon between the time we got home from morning church and before we went to evening church, Kent and his friends were playing croquet on our front lawn. They were laughing and arguing good-naturedly and secretly moving their ball ahead to cheat just a little bit. They were having a great time.

I was standing on the front porch enjoying watching them when one of them invited me to join the game. I was thrilled that I would soon be playing with these older fellows. I felt proud as I picked up a mallet and a wooden ball and joined in the fun. I had the time of my life playing with those guys. I hoped some of my friends would drive by our place with their parents or ride by on their bicycles and see me playing with older guys.

About half and hour before it was time for me to go to church, my brother Kent and his three friends decided to go for a ride in Moe Murdoch's Model A Ford. Moe was the only one in the whole school who had a car. I was disappointed when Moe announced, "We can't go, because my car's about out of gas, and I haven't got any money to buy any more."

Kent spoke up and said, "I think George has some money. Haven't you got some brown egg money, George?"

I didn't know how to answer, because I sure didn't want to spend any of my money. Kent said, "George, if you'll give us just a dollar, we will let you ride around with us."

My heart started to pound as I considered how it would be to ride around in that Model A with those older guys.

But then I sadly realized that it was nearly time to walk to church with my mother. I took a few steps toward the porch to go in the house and put on my suit. But when I went up the first porch step I thought, *I'll probably never get another chance to ride around town in the Model A with these older guys. Besides, I could miss church just this one time.*

I didn't know what to do. I stood there not going either up the stairs or down them. Kent spoke up and said, "Go get a dollar."

I replied, "Church starts in twenty minutes. Will we be back by then?"

"Of course we won't be back by then," Kent replied. "Hurry up and go get the dollar."

I raced in the house, got the dollar, and was headed out the door when my mother asked, "Where are you going?"

"I'm going to go riding around in the Model A with Kent and his friends."

I was still on the move when mother shouted, "Who will go to church with me?"

I replied, "Mom you're just going to have to learn to go to church by yourself."

Before Mom could say more, I was out the door. And thirty seconds later I was in the coveted back seat of Moe Murdoch's Model A Ford. I felt like I was in heaven.

I handed Moe the dollar. We went down to Kelly's service station and bought three gallons of gasoline.

For more than an hour we rode up and down the streets in American Fork from the shores of Utah Lake to the mouth of the canyon.

I didn't say a word the whole time. I let the older guys do all the talking and laughing. I just sat there feeling good. I felt like I was a king in a golden carriage. I sat with my nose close to the window so that if we passed anyone I knew they could see that I was with these older guys driving around American Fork in Moe Murdoch's Model A.

I was bitterly disappointed when we did not pass a single person that I knew. No one would be able to tell the other kids at school that they saw George riding around with the older guys in the Model A.

Finally, they decided we should head for home. As fate would have it, we passed by the old Fourth

Ward meetinghouse just as church was letting out. I looked at the door of the building that led ten or more cement steps down to the sidewalk.

It was a terrible coincidence. But just as we passed the meetinghouse, I saw my mother coming down those stairs holding onto the rail. I hoped she wouldn't stumble.

All the joy went out of heart. I wanted to shout, "Stop the car! I want to get out!" But I didn't have the courage to do that.

We continued to our house, and Kent and I went in. He hurried to his bedroom, but I waited in the kitchen for Mom to come home.

Twenty minutes later she came in the front door of our large kitchen. I was sitting over in the corner, acting like I was reading a book. When she was halfway in the door, I looked up. I'll never forget how she looked at me. I can still see the hurt in her eyes. I didn't know what to say.

I finally stood and walked a little closer to her and said, "Mother you'll never go to church alone again as long as I'm alive."

She came over and sat in the rocking chair, and I sat on her lap. As we gently rocked back and forth, I decided for myself that the next week Herbie and I would be there to prepare the sacrament as we had done in the past. Then, after church, I would be there to walk down the stairs, holding on my mother's arm so she wouldn't fall.

Chapter Eleven

George's Aaronic Priesthood days were filled with having to make a multitude of decisions. During that critical time, he made some good decisions as well as some that were not so good.

George told one story about an experience where he some poor choices and then one really good one. Two months after his fishing trip with Kent, he walked down the old Mill Lane, climbed up the hill, and entered the school for the first day of ninth grade. He was glad to see his old friends as he walked down the hall. He liked the social part of school better than he liked the studying part. He was one of those guys who didn't take schoolwork too seriously.

George reached in his pocket, pulled out his class schedule, and headed for the first classroom. One of the highlights of his day was always gym class, but that wasn't until fourth period. As he went from class to class for the first two hours, he was saddened to see that Louise was not among the students there. But when he went to his third class, there she was, and she looked even more beautiful than ever.

She looked at George as he walked in. She smiled and said an almost silent, "Hello."

He immediately knew that third hour would be his favorite class.

On that first day, Miss Isom said, "I don't want to call roll every day. So we're going to have a seating chart. That way I can just look at the empty seats and know who is missing."

George couldn't believe his good fortune when he learned he was seated right behind Louise. Truly this would be his best school year so far.

As the school year progressed, George was a little sad each day as he walked to school knowing the long hours he would have to spend in the uncomfortable seats listening to what he considered to be boring lectures. But when he thought that in third hour he would see Louise's blonde hair and blue eyes, his heart was gladdened.

George never told anyone how he felt about Louise. He was afraid they would say, "You can like Louise all you want, but she could never like a dud like you."

So he just kept his feelings about Louise—his fondest feelings by far—to himself.

George recalls an experience he had in that class:

> Friday was the only day Mrs. Isom called the roll. She did so on that day so that each student could respond when their name was called. If they were prepared to report on a current event during the class period, they said, "Prepared," If they didn't want to give a report, they said, "Unprepared."
>
> I quickly learned that Mrs. Isom was the kind of teacher who didn't make you do anything. She said it was up to us. We had free agency: if we wanted to do the work, we could, but if we didn't want to do the work, we didn't have to.
>
> But she always added this terrifying message: "If you don't do the work, you will get a grade that will show your parents that you did not do the work."
>
> Each Friday when Mrs. Isom called the roll, I was smart enough to know that if I said

"Unprepared" I wouldn't have to give a talk. I didn't want to give a talk, because some of the guys in the class always laughed at the speakers. I knew about that humiliating laughter because I was one of those who would laugh at the students who were giving talks. So each Friday when she called my name, I answered, "Unprepared."

I got so I could say that word with quite a bit of dignity. I sat up straight and said, with authority, "Unprepared."

My supportive friends always nodded their approval of my answer. This went on for a couple of months, so I had said "Unprepared" at least eight times.

Then one day Mrs. Isom called me to the front and showed me what was in her roll book. There I saw my name, *George Durrant,* and following my name were eight minus signs. She explained to me that those minus signs would transform into an F, and I would have to take that home to my mom and dad.

As I pondered my predicament, I considered the humiliation I would feel when I showed my parents my bad grade. But that embarrassment would be far less than the humiliation I would feel from the ridicule of my peers if I gave a talk.

I was saddened to hear this news regarding my impending grade, but I just didn't have the courage to give one of those talks.

The next Friday I once again said the predictable word: "Unprepared."

I did this for two more Fridays—two more minus signs in the role book.

The next week, as usual, I was sitting behind Louise. I never talked to her. I just didn't have the confidence to say any more to her other than "Hello," after which I quickly looked away.

That day Mrs. Isom called the roll, and I answered "Unprepared." To my surprise, Louise turned around and looked at me.

I quickly looked down at my desk. I looked to the right. But I could tell Louise was still looking at me. You can tell when somebody is looking at you. I quickly turned my head and looked to the left. Then I looked up at the ceiling. Finally I didn't know where else to look. I was compelled to look straight ahead.

I looked right into the eyes of Louise. I'll never forget what she said. She glared at me and asked in an uncharacteristically stern tone, "George, why don't you get prepared?"

Then she turned around and looked straight ahead. I looked down at my hands. My fingers were interlocked across my desk, and my knuckles were white. In the minutes that followed, I asked myself, *What does she care? Unless she cares.*

After school that day, I cut an article out of the newspaper about American bombers destroying an enemy battleship in the war that was raging at that time. I read the article, which was several paragraphs long. I read it again and again.

Finally, I could remember every word without even looking at it—I had it memorized.

I was motivated.

I carried the article in my wallet all week. Each day I read it again.

Finally, it was Friday, third hour. Mrs. Isom started calling the roll. She didn't look up because she didn't want to put the plus or negative sign on the wrong line.

She called those names that began with A, then B, and then C. My heart pounded faster as she got closer to the Ds. I was tempted to fall back into my old pattern and answer "Unprepared." But it was too late for that.

The sound that formed the name *George!* reverberated back and forth on the four walls of the classroom.

Miss Isom, without looking up from the roll, quickly marked the negative sign before I could reply, because she knew I'd say the same thing I had always said. I remained silent for a few seconds. The noise that was always present in the classroom was suddenly stilled by my silence. Finally, I took a deep breath and quietly said, "Prepared."

A shock rippled through the classroom. My friends stared at me in disbelief and wanted to shout out, "Traitor!" I had destroyed our unity. We had always supported one another, but now, to their dismay, I had broken away.

Mrs. Isom sat up straight when she heard my answer. She held her pencil in place but lifted her eyes to look at me. She stared as if I had just ruined her day. I stared back and then nodded my head.

Louise turned around and looked at me. This time I did not look away. As she faced me, a half smile crossed her face and she nodded her head slightly. She then turned and looked straight ahead, but to me she was still staring into my eyes

Mrs. Isom struck her pen across the negative sign and made it into a plus.

But then the glory was over, and the agony set in. I asked myself, *What have I done? Now I have to get up there and give the talk and be humiliated by my friends. I should have said "Unprepared."*

But it was too late now. The ten or so students who had answered "Prepared" had already given their talks. Miss Isom had saved me for last.

My hands shook and my heart pounded as she finally she looked at me as if to ask, "Are you really going to do this, George?"

I knew I had to do it. I stood up. I felt the eyes of thirty students and one teacher all focused on me.

I made the seemingly long walk to the front of the room. My back was to the students. I didn't dare turn around. But I knew I had to.

I looked out at what seemed like ten thousand faces. I gulped. And then I began to speak. I remembered the first word, the first line. Somehow the feelings of fear departed. I remembered the first paragraph. I remembered the whole thing—every word.

When I said that last word, I just stood there. I did not want to return to my seat. I wanted to say more. It seemed like the dam that was holding me back had been breached, and the water of confidence was free to flow.

I decided not to walk back to my seat. Instead, I decided to fly. When I approached Louise, I hovered over her like a helicopter. She looked up at me and smiled. I collapsed into my seat.

I said to myself, This is the only way to live. I'm always going to be prepared. I'm going to do good stuff.

That day I took Mrs. Isom's free agency from her. She had to change the sign by my name from a negative sign to a plus sign.

Somehow when she did, the negative signs in my heart also automatically switched to pluses.

I wish I had a microfilm of that roll book. It was one of the great records of my life.

That day when I knew I had done the right thing, I had the same kind of feelings I always had at church when Herbie and I passed the sacrament to the people I loved.

But life is a little bit like a war. Just because you win one battle doesn't mean you will win the next or the next. I was still a struggling student, but after that I knew that if I really tried, I could do it. I could be prepared."

The feelings I had that day weren't like the fun feeling I had being at Lagoon or an amusement park. They were a different kind of feeling. It was the kind of feeling I had when I made a basket in basketball, which I seldom did. It was a feeling of joy.

Well, what do you think? It looks like George might turn out to be a permanently religious guy. He might decide for himself to keep attending church. Maybe he will soon become a priest in the Aaronic Priesthood.

Let's see what happens next.

Chapter Twelve

By this time, George had completed more than one year as a teacher in the Aaronic Priesthood. Other than that one Sunday, when he was riding around in the Model A, he was always at church to partner with Herbie in their sacramental duties.

George was now fifteen years old, and it was his first day of school as a sophomore.

He recalled:

As I walked up the hill and into the school, I was greeted by my best friend, a guy I'll call Jeff. Jeff and I had been classmates from the first grade on. He was sort of everything I wanted to be. He had broad shoulders, wavy blonde hair, and all the girls liked him best. He was a great athlete. I felt it was an honor for me to be his friend.

After a whole summer, we were glad to see each other and compare schedules to see if we were in any of the same classes. I was surprised to hear him say, "I hate this place. I would give anything if I didn't have to come to school." Then he asked, "Do you hate being here as much as I do?"

"Well," I said hesitantly, "I don't like it a whole lot, but, you know, I don't hate it or anything like that."

He didn't seem to hear what I said as he continued his rant. "Man! I can't stand it here. I don't think there's a good teacher in the whole place, and the things they make us learn are never going to do us any good. I wish I could just get out of here and get a job and a car."

Just then the bell rang, and we went our separate ways. As I walked up the stairs to the second floor, I kept thinking about Jeff. I wondered what was going on with him. He always seemed to like school before.

As I hurried to my first classroom, I saw a multitude of students going both directions. I hardly recognized some of the guys because they had matured so much. So had the girls.

It seemed like the world was changing for all of us sophomores. I was little bit shocked when I heard some swear words I had never heard in the halls of the school before.

At the conclusion of the last hour of school, all us boys who longed to be athletes headed for the gymnasium. We knew Coach Nelson was going to issue football uniforms to those he thought had potential in that sport. I stood there with the rest of the sophomore guys waiting for the coach to come out of his office. I hoped that he would somehow hand some football gear to me. But I realized that would be a miracle, as there were so many other guys bigger and stronger than I was. But I still hoped. I was pretty good at hoping.

In those days, sophomores usually didn't get to be on the varsity football team. And there wasn't a sophomore team. Because of that, Coach Nelson had only a few secondhand outfits to distribute.

We all followed the coach into the locker room where the equipment was. There he began to call out the names he had written on a piece of paper. He read each name and then handed out the pads, pants, shirts, and cleats to the boy whose name he had called.

I expected, and I think Jeff did also, that his name would be among the first to be called. But that was not the case. After three names had been called. he started to fidget. After five names had been called and Jeff's name was not among them, he turned to me and said, "Tell old Nelson that if he wants me to play football, I'm out in the hall." With that, he turned and left.

Busy handing out the gear, the coach did not see Jeff leave. The next name he called was "Jeff."

He looked around, and then looking at me he asked, "Where's your buddy, Jeff?"

After a slight hesitation, I replied, "He's out in the hall."

The coach abruptly said, "Go tell him if he wants to play football to get back in here."

I hurried to the hall, and saw Jeff standing with one foot cocked back against the wall. He was talking to a couple of other guys. I excitedly told him, "The coach called your name. He said that if you want to play football to get back in there."

Jeff was chewing gum, and between his chomps he said, "Tell the coach to go to—"

Shocked, I replied, "You'll have to do that yourself."

Jeff never did play football. His big hands never threw a forward pass to win a game for our school.

As the weeks went on, I observed that Jeff and some of the other guys skipped classes and went down to the east side of campus to the little bridge that crossed the old mill stream, where they smoked cigarettes.

I tell the story of Jeff to illustrate that we were all at the age where changes were happening. Our bodies and even our souls seem to be different than they had been. We were growing up.

We had never had any experience what with what was called "maturing." We were not too good at adjusting to that because we had never done something that dramatic before. And we were not too good at adjusting to the new stuff that was going on inside us and all around us. It seemed like we didn't quite know how to handle it all.

Not all of us changed as much as Jeff did. But we all changed—not only in our physical bodies, but also in our inward feelings, feelings that affected our attitude about life and religion and stuff like that. I was also caught up in these changes, and it was a little more difficult for me to be a "good boy."

Three years older than I, Kent had drifted further and further away from the Church. He got married between his junior and senior year of high school. In his senior year, he was in the beginning stages of alcoholism. He still played basketball, but the stardom he was destined to attain was curtailed. He won an athletic scholarship, but he had no interest in going to college.

Sadly, I still had a slight yearning to be like him.

I didn't want to continue to be what Kent had called "a mama's boy—a sissy." Don't get me wrong. I wasn't a bad boy. But I considered becoming a bit more rebellious than I had been.

I still wanted to Jeff's friend, but that meant I would be hanging around guys who were swearing and smoking and stuff like that. I sort of wanted to do that, but I somehow just didn't have that kind of stuff in me.

I did skip classes once in a while, but I didn't go down to the bridge where the smokers were. I just went down to Abel's Store and bought myself a candy bar or a popsicle or something like that. Sometimes I was little rowdy in my classes. I even started using a couple of minor swear words.

On the brighter side, my mom used to always greet me at the front door when I came from school. As soon as I came in the door, she asked if I was hungry. I always said, "Yes." That's because in those days I was always hungry.

She smiled at my answer and sliced off a thick piece of homemade bread, covered it with home-churned butter, and topped it off with a thin layer of Skippy peanut butter. My mouth watered as she went through this daily ritual.

After handing me the delicacy, she always took her seat in the rocking chair. And I sat on her lap and savored my tasty treat. I gulped it down so fast that it hardly had time to stick to the roof of my mouth. When it was finished, I always said, "Mom, stuff always tastes better when you make it for me."

I sat on her lap and ate peanut butter sandwiches when I was a little kid, and as I got older, I never stopped. Of course, when I was in high school, I didn't sit on her lap until I had first pulled the drapes so nobody could look in and see me sitting on my mom's lap.

I remember the seemingly thousands of times when we sat there and she ran her fingers through my hair and told me I was special. I wondered why the girls didn't know that and why the coaches didn't know that. But I always believed her. I knew I was special, but I also knew I could not quite be that special.

One day I came home from school and she wasn't there to greet me. As I entered the motherless kitchen, I could hear talk coming from our front room. I moved to the half-open door and could see that Mom was in there with some other women making a quilt.

I knew there was no way I could interrupt something that important, and I realized I had to make my own sandwich.

I awkwardly cut a slice of homemade bread that was too thin on one end and too thick on the other. I quickly applied a gob of butter in the center and tried to smooth it around, but it didn't flatten out like it was supposed to. Impatiently, I scooped some hardened peanut butter from the nearly empty bottle with the kitchen knife and tried to cover the butter. What I had created looked more like a pinto horse than it did a peanut butter sandwich.

I sat in the empty rocking chair and began to eat my creation. But for some reason, it just did not taste right.

After I finished eating my sandwich, I stealthily made my way over to the half-open door so I could hear more clearly what the ladies were saying.

They were talking about all the bad things the boys were doing up at the high school. My mother didn't say anything until they had all stopped talking. Then she said, "I don't know if all the boys up at the school are doing the bad things you say. All I know is that my son George isn't doing those things."

When she said that, I said to myself, *I'm going to stop doing all those things.*

Even though I was changing sometimes toward the bad, I was still greatly influenced toward the good by my mother.

There were other factors that drew me toward good choices. One of them was Herbie, who never seemed to do a bad thing in his whole life—and he was my church buddy.

There was still the sacrament to be prepared and passed. And I still had a desire to be like my brother, the bishop, who was regarded in town as the finest of all men. Many said that through his priesthood he had the gift of healing. I wondered if I would ever have such a gift from God. Deep down in my heart, I wanted to be like him.

And there was my Sunday school teacher, Cliff Young. He was a banker. He was such a good teacher. It seemed to me that he was personally acquainted with Jesus. He told us how Jesus drove the moneychangers out of the temple. I almost cheered when he told us how Jesus always got the best of the evil scribes and Pharisees who tried to trick Him. And Jesus was so smart He could make them eat their words. Because of Brother Young, Jesus was kind of my personal hero.

It was a strange thing, but even though I was struggling with school and life, I thought about

Jesus a lot of the time. He had a real influence on me. I never told nobody about that.

I still didn't know much about Joseph Smith. I could faintly recall what my Primary teacher, Laura Timpson, told me about him going to the trees and seeing God and Jesus. She called it the First Vision.

In a couple of my Sunday school classes, we talked about the same thing. I remember thinking, *It must be real, or my teachers wouldn't be talking about it so much.*

Regarding Joseph Smith's First Vision, something strange happened to me the summer before my junior year in high school. I was down south of town at the plot of ground my father had rented so that he and I could grow an acre of celery. He thought we would make a lot of money doing that, but we didn't

Anyway, I was down there all by myself irrigating the fast-growing celery plants. A rainstorm started, complete with thunder and lightning.

Before I knew it, I was knocked out by a bolt of lightning. A neighboring farmer who saw all happen came rushing over. He saw me laying there, half in the water and half out.

He thought I was a goner, but he shook me and woke me up. He asked me if I was all right. I had mud in my ears and in my hair, but I was not burned or anything like that, and I suffered no ill effects from the experience.

After that my older brothers would laughingly tease me by saying, "I don't think you were hit by lightning. I just think you had a vision just like Joseph Smith did."

We all laughed at that, but later I started thinking, *I wish I could have a vision like Joseph Smith had.* But no such thing ever happened to me.

My conviction about Joseph Smith being a prophet and stuff like that was kind of like a tulip bulb planted in the ground when I was young. A tulip didn't pop out of the ground at that time.

We have learned some of the pushes and pulls of George's spiritual life by the end of his sophomore year. He was a bit like a basketball when the jump ball was called. The ball was going to be thrown between good and evil, and it wasn't quite known which way the ball would be tipped. Maybe the ball would be tipped to the bad court, or maybe it would be tipped to the good court.

Which way do you think things will go for George? Let's find out.

During the school year, George made the sophomore basketball team, but his classmates and the local sports fans compared him to his older brother Kent. Kent was a superstar; George was not even a super sub. Kent was a giant, and George's growth seemed stunted.

He had grown an inch or so, but his original navy-blue suit he was given at the age of twelve still fit him. He prayed to grow. But figured that his mother, who could only afford one suit, was praying that he wouldn't. Her prayers were always more powerful than his own.

George's unanswered dream to be as tall as Kent was a constant source of pain to the uncertain young man.

Louise was still there. Her friendly "Hellos" each day did much to keep him going. George felt that the only reason Louise was in the school was because Heavenly Father knew that George needed her.

Chapter Thirteen

A month after beginning his junior year in high school, George turned sixteen years old. It was time for him to become a priest in the Aaronic Priesthood.

Bishop Grant, his new bishop, took George aside after Sunday school to schedule a time when he could be ordained to that new office.

George advised the bishop that perhaps he was not ready to be a priest. When the bishop asked why, George reported, "Sometimes I, like some of my teammates in the locker room, use swear words. I don't do it too often. But sometimes I do."

The bishop encouraged George to change his ways. He felt George's sins were not too serious and that becoming a priest would help him do even better.

After that discussion, George agreed that the bishop could proceed with the ordination the next Sunday.

Seven days later as George entered the chapel, the bishop told him that the ordination would take place right after Sunday school. The bishop wanted George to tell his mother so she could be there.

During Sunday school, George's mind was in a state of wonderment. He asked himself whether he was really worthy to be a priest. He answered his own question by thinking, *I guess if the bishop thinks I'm worthy, I might be.* Then he hoped he could quit using swear words.

After Sunday school, George hurried to be the first to arrive in the bishop's office. The bishop arrived next, and George pleaded, "Could we keep the door closed for a few minutes? There's something else I want to talk to you about."

The bishop closed the door behind him and said, "Sure. What's on your mind?"

While the two were still standing, George shook his head, ran his hand through his hair, and said, "It's just . . . It's just that I . . . I don't know. I don't think I can memorize that long prayer that the priests say when they bless the bread and water."

The bishop replied, "You don't have to memorize it, George. You just read it. You can do that, can't you?"

George answered, "I can read it, but not when everyone in the chapel is listening."

Bishop Grant's next words were mingled with laughter. "George, I love you. You're one of the finest, most honest guys I've ever known. The Lord will bless you. With His help, there's nothing you can't do."

Just then there was a knock on the door. The bishop opened the door, and George's mother walked in. So did Herbie Pawlowski and his parents.

Herbie was first to be ordained, and then it was George's turn. The bishop laid his hands on George's head and ordained him to be a priest in the Aaronic Priesthood of The Church of Jesus Christ of Latter-day Saints. While he was still talking, the bishop added these words to the blessing: "Dear Heavenly Father, bless George with the knowledge that whatever You ask him to do, he will be able to do."

Following the ordination, George stood up, shook hands with the bishop, and looked into his leader's eyes. Any doubts he had about becoming a priest were erased from his mind.

George was finally growing taller. So during that next week, George's mother took him to Devey's Men's Store, where they bought George a brand-new navy-blue suit so he would look like a priesthood man as he began his career as a priest.

Chapter Fourteen

The next Sunday, George was greeted at the front door by his compatriot Herbie Pawlowski. The two made their way solemnly to the sacrament table. George's mother had made her way to the front row to be as close to her adored son as she could be.

The opening song was sung. The opening prayer was said. The announcements were made. The organist began to play the hymn. The congregation began to sing, "Oh it is wonderful, that He should care for me enough to die for me."

It was time.

George and Herbie stood in unison, reached out, took the corners of the white cloth in hand, and uncovered the sacrament trays. The two young priesthood holders then began to break the slices of bread into the sacrament trays.

Of this experience, George reported:

> I knew just the right size pieces in which to break the bread. I looked down while I was performing this sacred task because I hardly dared look up to see all the folks singing and staring at me. Finally, the bread was broken. Herbie spoke softly, "Do you want to do the bread?"
>
> "I do."
>
> I adjusted the card so I could see it perfectly. I cleared my throat. I lowered my voice an octave so I would sound more spiritual.

I read the first words, "Oh God, the Eternal Father. . . ." When I said those holy words, all fear left my heart. I continued, with no mistakes, to the final "Amen."

George stood, and he and Herbie handed the trays across the sacrament table to the new deacons. George humbly hoped that somehow those new deacons could perform the sacred duties as well as he and Herbie had.

As the Deacons went their way, Herbie and George sat down. A feeling of goodness overcame George. He was overwhelmed by what he had just been able to do. Involuntarily, he looked at his mother. She was shedding tears of joy. He looked around the chapel, and everyone was looking at him—not in derision, but in admiration. He felt that at that moment that he had become the real George Durrant. He later realized it was the most spiritual and joyous moment of his entire life.

During his junior and senior years in high school, George recalled:

I blessed the sacrament each Sunday. Each week as I broke the bread, I thought to myself, *The hands that are used to break this sacred bread can never be used to hold a can of beer or a cigarette or do other unholy things.*

In my better moments, I thought, *The tough guys are not the ones up the canyon drinking beer. The tough guys are down in the Valley doing their priesthood duties.*

George didn't always think these lofty thoughts as he participated in the sacrament. But he knew that those were the very thoughts that enabled him to live in a more respectable way as he negotiated the difficult years of high school.

Chapter Fifteen

During the summer before his senior year in high school, George dreamed that his senior year would be the year during which he would really blossom. He would be chosen as senior class president. He would make All State in basketball. And he would be popular with the girls.

George felt that reaching each of these goals would form the foundation for what he really wanted. And what he really wanted was to be known as a "big wheel." When people saw him, he wanted them to say, "There's George, and he is a big wheel."

George's goals sound pretty impressive, don't you think?

Let's have George tell us in his own words how he did in reaching those goals:

My first goal was to be senior class president. Unfortunately for me, the students did not know what a good leader I was, so I was never nominated to be class president. And because I was never nominated, of course I was never elected.

During football season I spent my time in the gymnasium practicing basketball. I had grown taller during the summer—I was six-foot-three, so I was big enough to achieve my All State status. But by Christmas we had played five games, and I had not been the star in any one of them.

Gradually I was relegated to the bench. I think that was because the coach liked me the best and wanted me near him on the bench all the time. It .is very difficult to make All State from the bench.

My goal to be popular with the girls was hinging upon me being All State. Girls like basketball players, but not the ones sitting on the bench. So saying I was popular with the girls would be quite an overstatement.

My only solace was that the best-looking girl in the school, the most popular girl in the school, the most academically gifted girl in the school was my girlfriend. She did not know she was my girlfriend, and I never told her. But I was the authority on that, and Louise was my girlfriend.

As my senior year progressed, I felt some general changes within myself. But I was still held back from radiating much of a personality by my shyness.

When I was a sophomore, I saw some of the guys who were juniors and seniors—bona fide big wheels—walking down the halls of the school with their arms around girls, talking and laughing. I looked on in envy and said to myself, *When I'm a junior, I'm going to do that.*

When I became a junior, I said to myself, *I'm going to wait until I'm a senior to do that.* I decided to put it off for two reasons. First, I was too timid to do that. And second, I couldn't find a girl who would go down the hall with my arm around her.

I believe that if you're really handsome in high school, Heavenly Father blesses you and makes you timid. I believe that's why I was timid.

Springtime came to American Fork, and there was only a month of school left. Knowing I should go on a date, I finally asked this girl to go with me to the movie. I was shocked when she agreed. I did not have a car, so I walked down to her house, and then the two of us walked three blocks to the Cameo Theater. As the two of us walked along, I could think of nothing to say, so I remained silent. So did she.

We entered the theater, and I saw the popcorn that was for sale. I bought a sack. I remember the name of the movie was *Sentimental Journey*. It was about as exciting as our lack of conversation with each other.

I nervously ate several handfuls of popcorn. I wondered if I should offer her some, but I was fearful that if I did she would say she didn't want any, and I didn't think I could stand such a rejection. So I ate whole sack of popcorn myself.

That was the beginning and ending of my date with that girl and every other girl.

It was now May, and the school year came to an end along with my high school career. It was the last day of school, and none of us went to class.

Four of my friends and I sat on the lawn near the big weeping willow tree that graced the front of dear old American Fork High School. As we sat there, the conversation between the four of us centered on what we were going to do now that we were out of high school. The others dreamed of getting a job, getting a car, and getting married. I really did not like any of those ideas, but I had hardly any idea of what I was going to do.

While we were talking, I felt the presence of someone standing above me. I looked up, and to my astonishment I saw Louise. She said, "George, I've been looking for you. I want to write in your yearbook. Could I do that?"

The other four in the group were even more surprised than I was at her presence and especially at the fact that she was paying attention to me. I'm sure they were thinking, *George is a dud. Why is this most popular girl in the school talking to him?*

I almost replied to Louise with as much boldness as I could must, "Sure you can write in my yearbook."

Louise's next words were, "I want to go somewhere where I can be alone to write. I might keep your yearbook for half an hour or so."

I replied, "You can keep it as long as you want, Louise."

I handed her the yearbook, and she walked away.

I tried not to give the impression to the other guys that I was a "big wheel," but I'm sure they sensed that I was.

For the next half hour or so, I wasn't much good at making conversation about the future because my mind was so consumed with the fact that Louise was somewhere alone writing in my yearbook.

Finally, she returned. She smiled as she said, "Thank you, George." As she handed me the book, it sort of fell open to where she had written. I quickly saw that her words had filled the whole page. Then as suddenly as she had appeared, she was gone.

I sensed that the other guys wanted to see what she had written. But I didn't think they were worthy to see what Louise had written in my book. I quickly closed the book.

Early that evening, I was alone in my back bedroom preparing to put on my best clothes—my navy-blue suit, a white shirt, and a red tie. I relished the thought that Louise would finally see me dressed in the clothes that I usually reserved for church activities. Surely she would think I was handsome.

Realizing that the graduation ceremony would take place an hour later, I sensed that it would be a good time to read what Louise had written.

My hands were trembling as I held the book, gently opened it, and thumbed through a few pages until I was looking at her message. Her writing was beautiful. Instead of putting a period mark above the all small letter is, she made a little circle. I said to myself, *I'm going to start doing that.*

I was shocked at her first words! I could scarcely believe my eyes: her first words were, "Dear George."

I whispered, "Why did she call me 'dear' unless . . ." I read again the words, "Dear George." After savoring these sacred words for a few seconds, I continued to read.

On the next line were the words, "I think you were the nicest boy in the senior class."

I stopped reading, lifted my eyes from the page, and looked toward the window. And had a tinge of regret. I did not want to be known as the "nicest boy." I wanted to be known as the most athletic boy. As the most popular boy. As a boy who was a "big wheel."

I did not want to be known as the nicest boy. I took a deep breath and read again the words, "I think you were the nicest boy in the senior class."

Somehow the words sounded different this time. A smile spread across my face as I said to myself, *I guess I am a pretty nice. I guess being nice is even better than some of the other things I wanted to be.*

I read on to see what else Louise had said: "I think you will go to college."

I shook my head from side to side, knowing there was little hope of that. I had barely made it through high school. But I considered her words and said to myself, *Maybe I will go to college. I never really tried in high school. Maybe I could go to college.*

Louise's next words shocked me: "I bet you will go on a mission for our church."

I put my hand on my forehead and rubbed it back and forth. With my eyes closed, I whispered, "I can't even hardly talk a girl into going out with me. How could I ever talk anyone into joining the Church?"

But then it seemed like someone had turned the lights on in the room as I remembered how I wondered if I could ever have the courage to say the prayer at the sacrament table. I did that. I love doing that. Maybe I will . . . maybe I will go on a mission.

The rest of Louise's writings were mainly about the memories we had shared in high school. After reading them I went back to the top of the page and read again the words, "Dear George."

I closed the book.

Her message was second in importance only to my patriarchal blessing, which I would receive later.

Chapter Sixteen

Well!

What do you think now? If George always follows these new goals, it appears he's setting himself up for a full life in the Church. But we all know things can happen. For George, there's still a distance to go.

Let's fast-forward and see what happens to George next.

George did go to college. He went to Brigham Young University. After one year there, George had another landmark experience in his religious life that ended his days in the Aaronic Priesthood.

Here's how George remembers that occasion:

> I received a phone call from the stake president, Phil D. Jensen. He invited me to come to his office that night for an interview.
>
> I was pretty nervous as I entered his office. I wondered what was about to happen. The president greeted me cordially and asked me to be seated.
>
> He advised me that something had just come up, and that he could spend only a few minutes with me. "So let's get right to it. I have a few questions I would like to ask you." He gazed at me as if he could see right through me. I squirmed in my chair.

"George," he continued, "do you smoke?"

I meekly responded, "No."

"Do you drink?"

"No."

"What about girls?"

I thought I knew what he meant, and replied, "I can't even get a date."

He then announced, "Well I've got to get going. But the reason I'm asking you these questions is, we would like to ordain you an elder. How would you like to be an elder?"

By now he was standing up and coming around the desk as he asked again, "What about it? Do you want to be an elder?

I replied, "I guess so."

As he turned to help me out the door, he announced, "Next Sunday is stake conference. We will present your name there. If the people sustain you, we will ordain you after the meeting." He turned to hurry away. As he looked over his shoulder, he said, "Is that all right, George?"

"Yeah. That would be all right."

In somewhat of a daze, I walked to my old car, turned on the key, pushed on the starter, and the motor roared to life. The car seemed to run better now that it knew I was getting more authority. As I drove out of the parking lot, a smile crossed my face. I was glad that I was going to become an elder.

I remembered that a week earlier an elder, a newly returned missionary, had spoken at a fireside. I could see how the young women were looking at him with great adoration. I wondered if I could ever speak like that and be like him. Then

I hopefully thought, "Maybe, when I'm an elder, maybe then."

As I pulled out on the main street, I felt glad that I was going to be an elder.

I aimlessly drove from where I was down to the other end of American Fork's business district. Then I made a U-turn and came back the other direction. That was something to do in American Fork.

I made another U-turn and drove down to the far end of the business district to Don's Sweetshop—a sweet shop owned by guy named Don. It was a place to have milkshakes and hamburgers and French fries. In those days there was no McDonald's or anything else like that in American Fork, so it was the place where all the young people gathered.

I parked my car and walked over to the doorway. I was wearing a navy-blue suit, my third one, because I had just talked to the stake president. I think I was glowing a little bit because I still thinking of the fact that I was going to become an elder.

I pushed the door open with a bit of gusto and took one step inside. There were booths all around the walls of Don's Sweetshop and some spin-around chairs up at the counter.

I noticed as I walked in the shop that all eyes turned and focused on me. I think it was because I was "looking good." Kinda like a big wheel. I wasn't necessarily good-looking, but right after you've talked to the stake president and when you're going to become an elder, you look good. I learned in a Book of Mormon class at BYU that you could get the name of Jesus Christ written in your heart and His image would appear in your countenance. I think all that was working that night when I entered Don's Sweetshop, because I could tell people thought I looked good.

I looked to my right and waved to the people sitting there as if I was the student-body president. Then I turned to the left and waved to those there. I was feeling pretty important.

I made my way up to the spin-around seats and sat down. There were three girls working there. Don always hired the prettiest girls in American Fork.

I noticed the girls seem to be pushing and shoving each other. It was then that I discovered they were doing that because each one wanted to wait on me. I had never had an experience like in my entire life. But I kinda liked what was happening.

Finally, one of the girls who was a little larger than the other two was able to push them aside and come and stand right across the counter from me. She asked me what I would like. I replied, "I would like a cherry chocolate milkshake with more cherry in it than chocolate."

She replied, "I know just how to make those. I'll make you a thick one, George."

As I sat there, I looked at a painting of some roses on the back wall. They looked real. I said to myself, *That's a good painting, and I painted it.* You see, I had begun to study art during the year I was at BYU.

Pretty soon the waitress brought me my milkshake. I started drinking it through a straw. I turned around every time I heard the door open, and I either said "Good night" or "Hello" to those who were going or coming. I felt like everybody would like a greeting from me. I had never felt that way before.

As I was drinking my milkshake, I got to thinking. The first thought I had was, *I'm as good as anybody else in this whole town.* Then I said to myself, *I'm no better than anybody else in this town.*

Then I had a good feeling and thought, *I'll bet I could amount to something if I really tried.*

About that time my milkshake started making noises that milkshakes make when they're gone. I stood up, and the three girls kind of looked at me longingly like, "George, if you stay around another half hour, I'll be getting off work and you can drive me home."

We used to do that in American Fork.

But I had places to go and things to do. I hated to disappoint the girls by leaving, but I wanted to get home.

I waved to the people on the right and on the left and told them goodnight. I went over to the door, turned back one last time, and waved again. I walked through the door out into the dark night of American Fork.

I think the people still in the sweetshop were wondering, "Who was that man?"

I drove home, parked the car, and went in my house. Mom and Dad had gone to bed early, so I was alone.

I went to my bedroom and knelt by my bed. I said something like, "Dear Father in Heaven, if you let me be an elder, I promise I'll try to be a good one. I'll never tell any more bad jokes. I'll never swear again." I made other promises to the Lord, but He didn't answer me. I went to sleep with a smile on my face.

The next week in a small room in the basement of the American Fork Tabernacle, John Pulley, a man holding the Melchizedek Priesthood and serving on the stake high council, came into the room where I sat with my mother. He laid his hands on my head and conferred upon me the Melchizedek Priesthood and ordained me an elder.

I've never gotten over the thrill of becoming an elder. After that day, I started writing my name *George D Durrant*. Now that I was an elder, I decided to add my middle initial.

Chapter Seventeen

Let's let George explain what happened next:

A year later, I went on a mission to England. I picked up the language just like that.

A month after I got to England I was asked to present at a district training meeting the lesson on the Restoration of the gospel. I prepared that talk in great detail. I wanted to impress the other missionaries as they impressed me.

I began to tell the story of Joseph Smith, just as my Primary teacher, Laura Timpson, had told it in my last year of Primary.

I told of young Joseph going to the Sacred Grove and asking Heavenly Father which church was true.

Something happened to me at that moment that changed my life. I was overcome with the emotion of pure joy. Sweet tears filled my eyes and ran down my cheeks. At first, I was embarrassed to be crying like that. But then I saw that the other seven missionaries were also in tears.

Between my sobs, I told of Joseph's persecutions. I told of his martyrdom.

I loved him. I knew Joseph Smith was a prophet of God.

My knees trembled as I walked back to my seat. My beloved companion, Elder Murray McInnis, rose from his chair, took me by the arm, and helped me to be seated. The bulb of truth that had been planted in my heart many years before by my mother and many faithful teachers had been nourished through the years, and it had now sprung up in its full glory to be the guiding light in my life.

As I sat there, I was a different man than I had ever been before. I knew there was a God in heaven. I knew that Jesus Christ was my Savior. I knew that the Book of Mormon was true. I knew the temple was a place to be married and that the gospel was the way to live.

Now, as I write this book many years later, I'm a high priest in The Church of Jesus Christ of Latter-day Saints.

My life is not over yet. I still have many things to do to try to repay the Lord for all He has done for me. It is my hope and dream that I will endure to the end.

Before I end this book, I want again to recall with you the conversation I had when I was a deacon with my brother Kent. You'll remember we were on a fishing trip to the South Fork of the Provo River.

We hadn't caught any fish, so we were talking on the banks of the river. We said many things on that occasion, but the thing I remember best was our conversation about whether I should continue to attend church. Let me remind you how that conversation went. Kent said, "George, you're a religious guy. You like going to church. Me, I don't like doing that. I don't see any sense in wasting my time over there when I'd sooner be somewhere else.

"When I don't go to Sunday school and that, Dad makes me clean out chicken coops. But I'd sooner do that than go to church and listen to boring talks and boring lessons. I'm just not interested in that kind of stuff. I don't want to pass the sacrament and stuff like that." He then looked at me and asked, "Do you like doing that kind of stuff?"

Before I even thought, I replied, "I kinda like doing that, but I been thinking maybe I could at least miss church some of the time. Then I could help you clean out chicken coops."

Kent stared at me until I had to look back at him. Then he said "Don't talk like that. If you didn't go to church, it would break Mom's heart. I know it makes her cry when I tell her I don't want to go to church. But I can't live my life just to please her. She likes going to church and thinks I should to, but I don't."

I felt all confused and didn't know what to say, so I just sat there looking at the river and thinking. Kent then said, "Some of my friends are like me and have quit going to church. The only ones who go are those who seem like 'mama's boys—kind of sissies—not the tough guys."

When I didn't answer him right off, Kent suggested, "You don't have to follow their example. And you don't have to follow mine. You just have to decide for yourself. Is it really worth going to church or not?"

That's the challenge I give to you: Is it really worth going to church or not?

Is it better to get up on Sunday morning and go to church, or is it better to go clean out a chicken coop?

The answer seems so simple when the alternative to church is to clean out a chicken coop. But forget the chicken coop—there are many alternatives to going to church that are very attractive. Things like sleeping in. Reading the Sunday paper. Watching athletic events on television. Going fishing. Playing sports. The list goes on and on. After all, there are far more attractive things than cleaning chicken coops.

I am so glad I decided to quit riding around in the Model A and to go over to the church and feel the Spirit of the Lord. I found out for myself that religion is the essence of the happiest kind of life.

I can't prove what I just said, but I know it's true.

Now you know the answer to the question that was asked at the beginning of the book: "As the years go by, will little George turn out to be religious or not?"

I'm sure glad the answer is, "He did."

I'll see you in church.